Other NEW YORKER *books*

The Art of *The New Yorker*, 1925—1995
by Lee Lorenz

The New Yorker Book of Doctor Cartoons

The New Yorker Book of Lawyer Cartoons

The New Yorker Book of Cat Cartoons

The Complete Book of Covers from *The New Yorker*,
1925—1989

THE NEW YORKER
BOOK OF DOG CARTOONS

THE
NEW YORKER
BOOK OF DOG CARTOONS

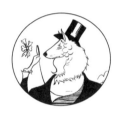

ALFRED A. KNOPF ❧ NEW YORK 2012

Copyright © 1992 by The New Yorker Magazine, Inc.

All rights reserved under International and Pan-American Copyright
Conventions. Published in the United States by Alfred A. Knopf, Inc.,
New York, and simultaneously in Canada by Random House of Canada
Limited, Toronto. Distributed by Random House, Inc., New York.

All the art is protected by registrations and renewals duly filed with
the Register of Copyrights, Library of Congress, by The New Yorker
Magazine, Inc., formerly the F-R Publishing Corp.

The magazine's name and logo are protected by registrations and
renewals duly filed with the Patent and Trademark Office, and in trademark
registries abroad.

All rights are reserved. No portion of this collection, nor any of its contents, may be
reproduced without the written consent of The New Yorker Magazine, Inc.

Library of Congress Cataloging-in-Publication Data

The New Yorker book of dog cartoons. — 1st miniature pbk. ed.
p. cm.
Includes index.
ISBN 0-679-76542-5
1. Dogs—Caricatures and cartoons. 2. American wit and humor, Pictorial.
3. New Yorker (New York, N.Y. : 1925) I. New Yorker (New York, N.Y. : 1925)
NC1428.N47 1995b
741.5′973—dc20
95-21555
CIP

Manufactured in Mexico
Published October 4, 1992
First Miniature Paperback Edition Published October 1995
Reprinted Eight Times
Tenth Printing, May 2012

THE
NEW YORKER
BOOK OF DOG CARTOONS

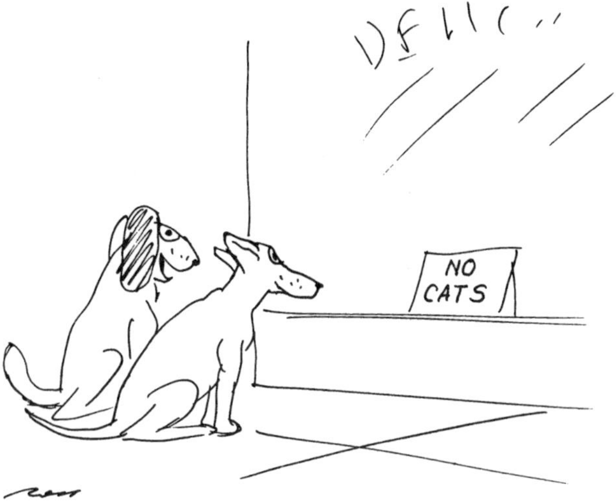
NO CATS

"Hey, the tide has turned!"

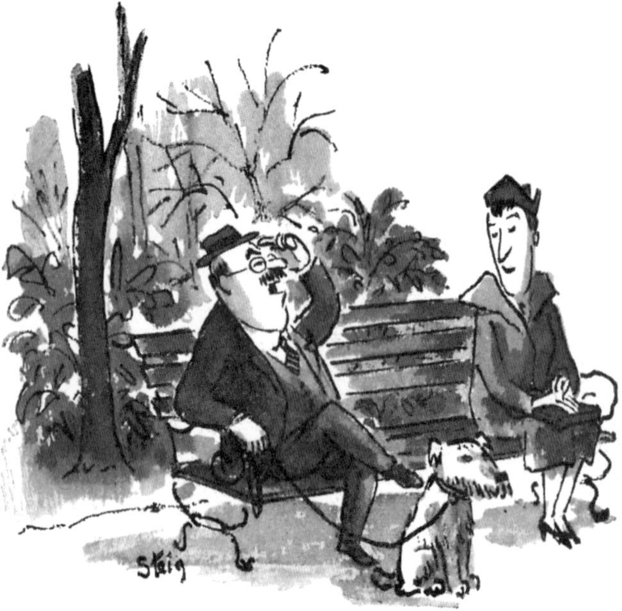
Steig

"Mongrels have it up here."

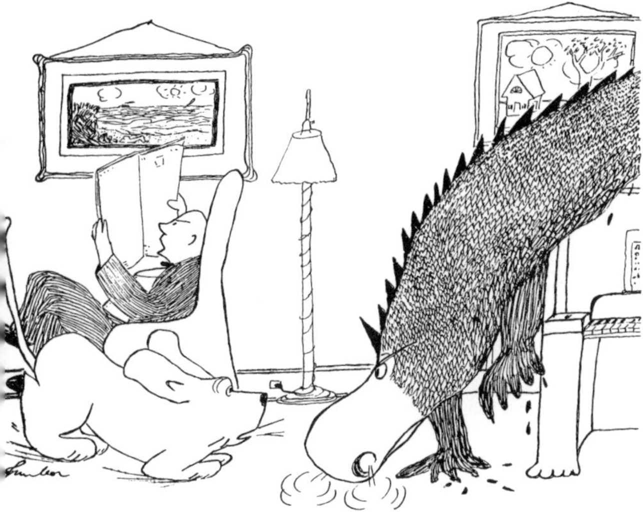

"Shut up, Prince! What's biting you?"

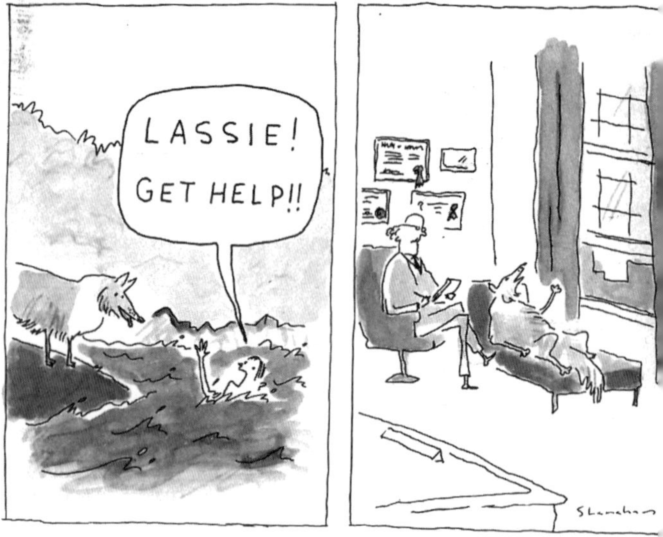
LASSIE! GET HELP!!
Shanahan

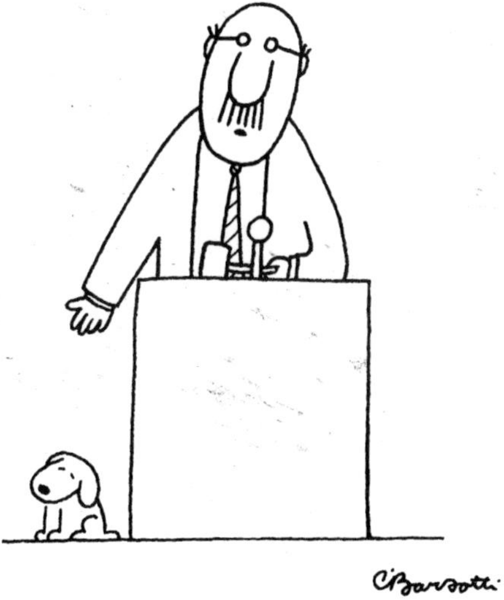
CBarsotti

"The bidding will start at eleven million dollars."

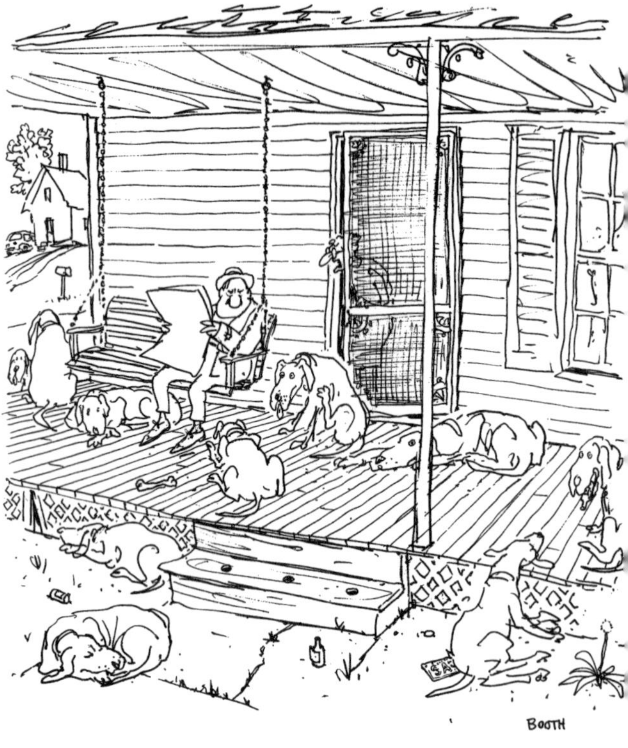
BOOTH

“Did you woof?”

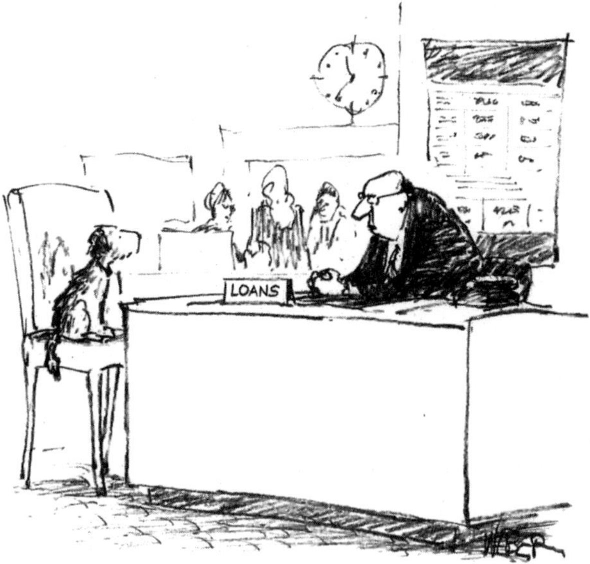
LOANS

"If you had an account here, it would be a different story."

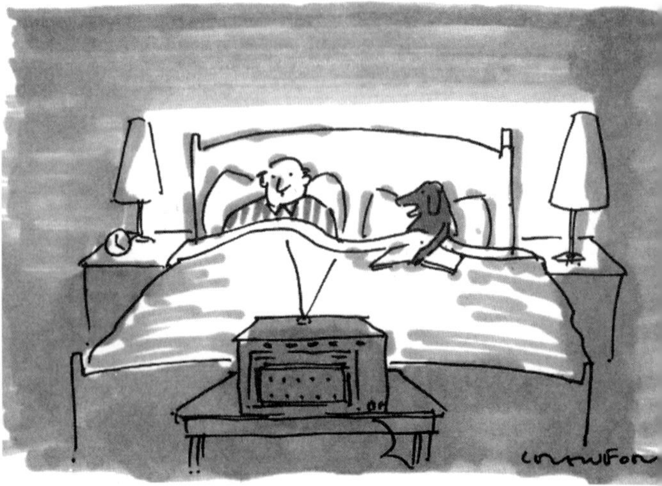

"Joe, I want out."

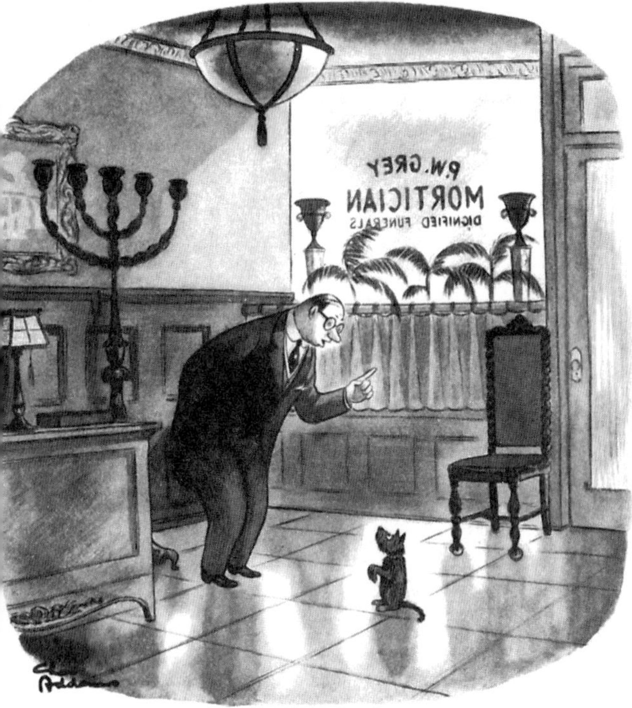
P.W. GREY
MORTICIAN
DIGNIFIED FUNERALS

"Now play dead."

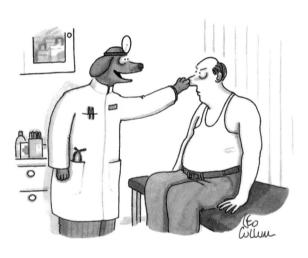

"Well, your nose feels cold."

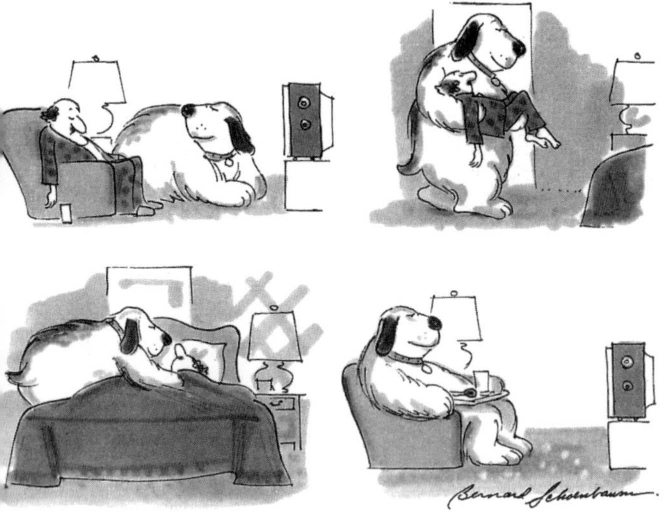
Bernard Schoenbaum

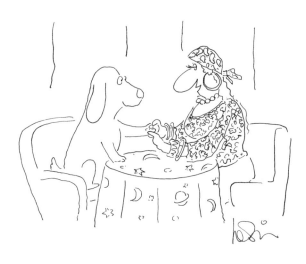

"*You will be going on a long walk.*"

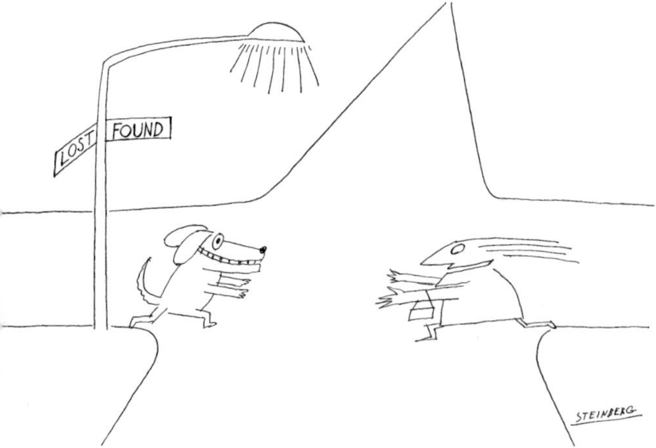
LOST
FOUND
STEINBERG

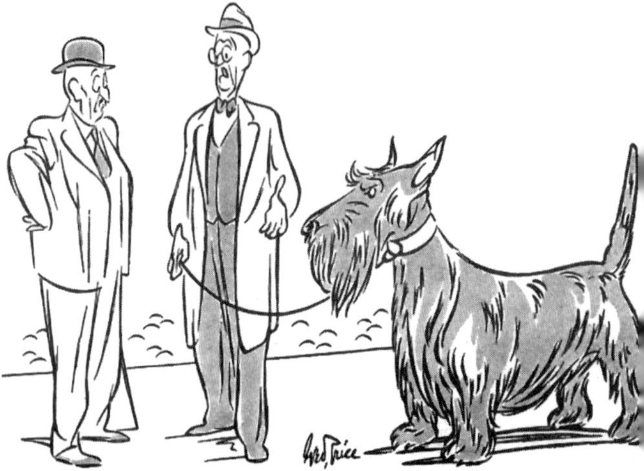

"We think it's a glandular disturbance."

IT'S TIME TO TREAT YOUR DOG TO

Le Bon Chien®

THE FIRST HAMBURGER-FLAVORED LIQUEUR FOR CANINES ONLY!

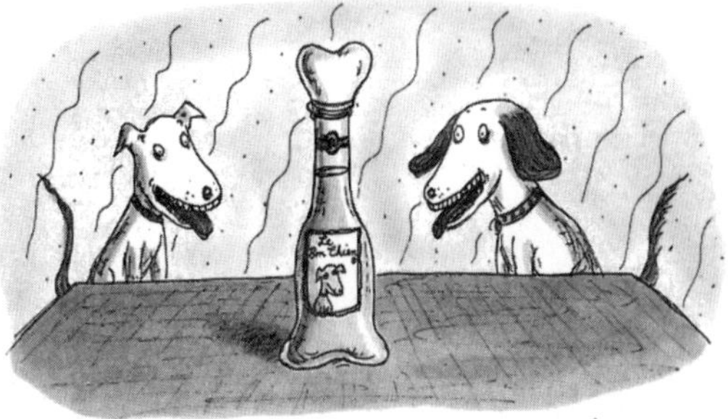
Le Bon Chien

Try serving Le Bon Chien® in any of these delightful ways:

"Fido"

Fill bowl with ice cubes. Pour 3 oz. Le Bon Chien® over ice. Serve.

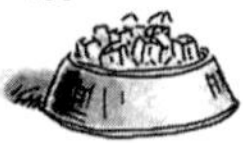

"Lassie in Reruns"

Mix 2 cups water with 1/4 cup Le Bon Chien® in bowl. Serve.

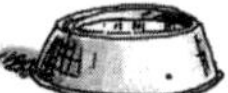

"101 Dalmatians"

Pour 12 oz. club soda into bowl. Add 3 oz. Le Bon Chien®. Float slice of bologna on top. Serve.

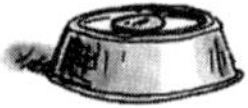

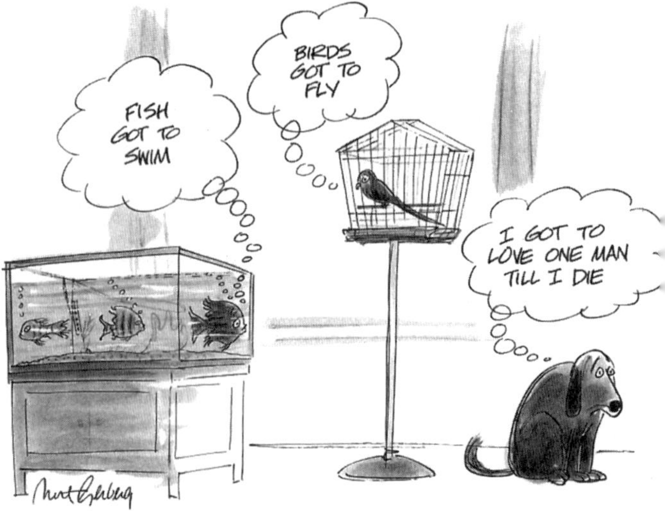
FISH
GOT TO
SWIM
BIRDS
GOT TO
FLY
I GOT TO
LOVE ONE MAN
TILL I DIE

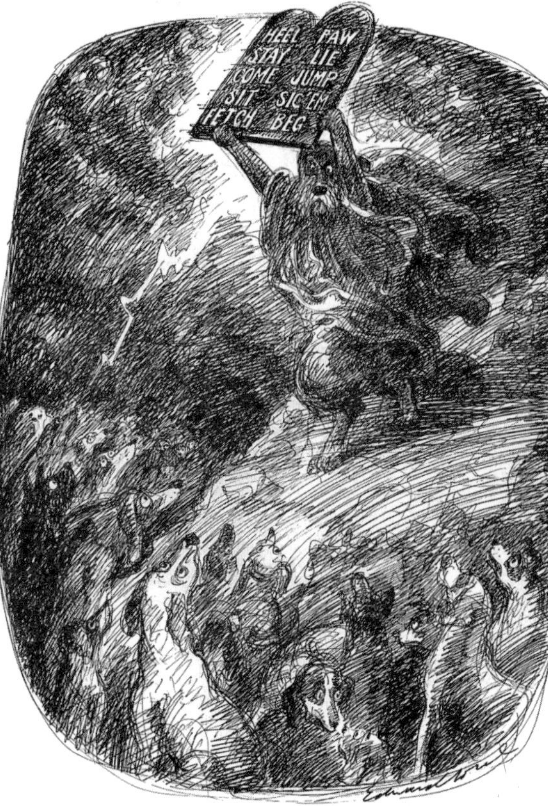
HEEL PAW
STAY LIE
COME JUMP
SIT SIC'EM
FETCH BEG

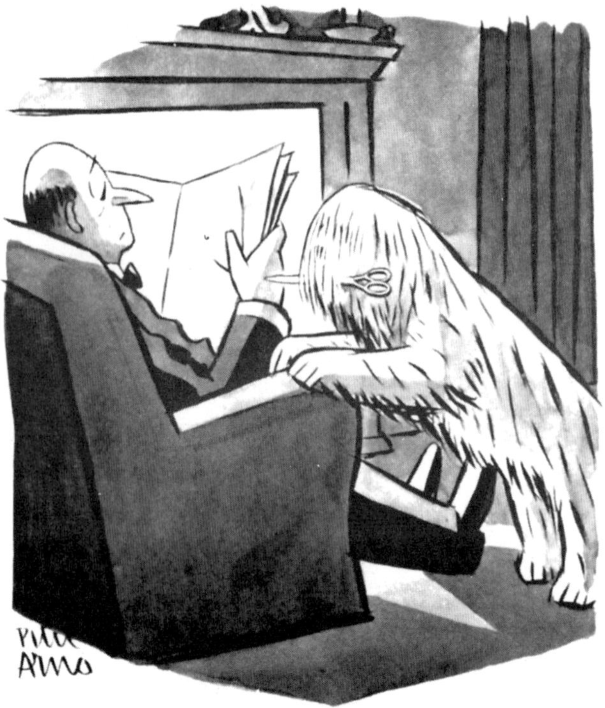
Peter
Arno

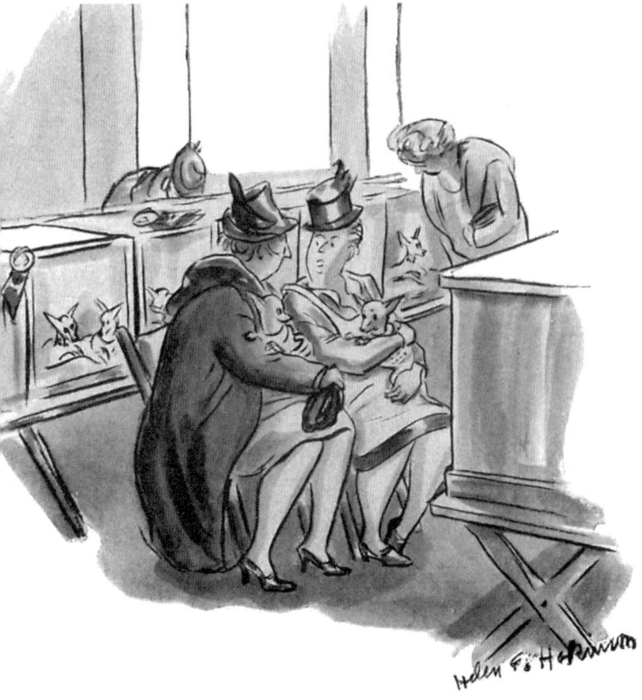
Helen E. Hokinson

"She's very like her father and has something of his sense of humor."

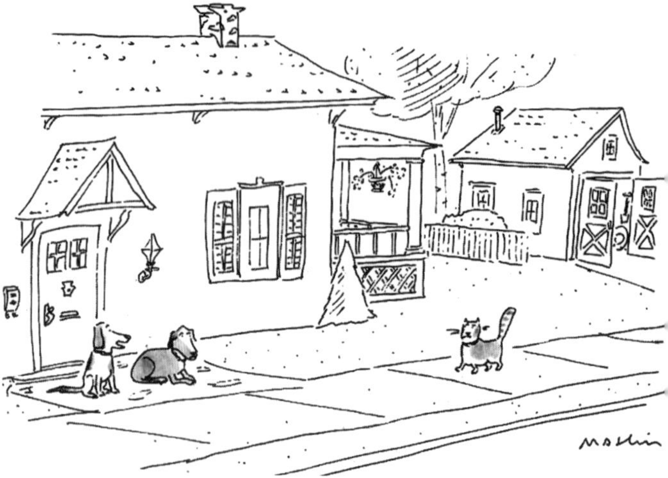
Maslin

"Do you want to handle this or should I?"

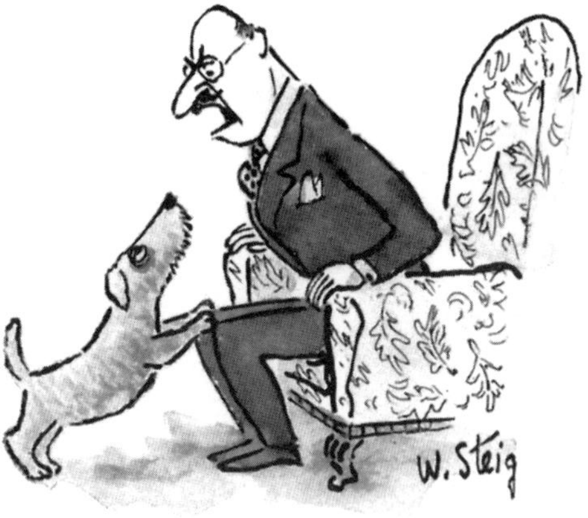
W. Steig

"Stop fawning!"

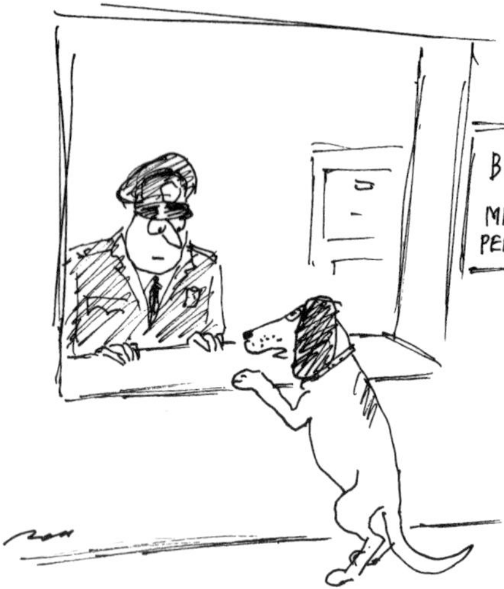
BUREAU
OF
MISSING
PERSONS

"He's about five feet six, has big brown eyes and curly blond hair, and answers to the name of Master."

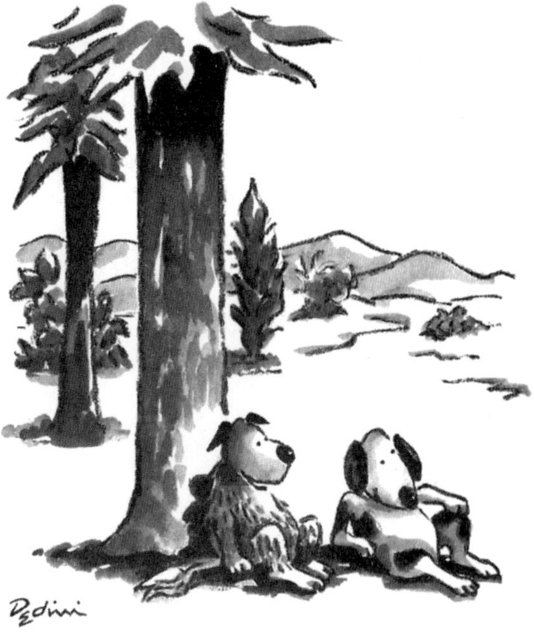

"We should get out to the country more often."

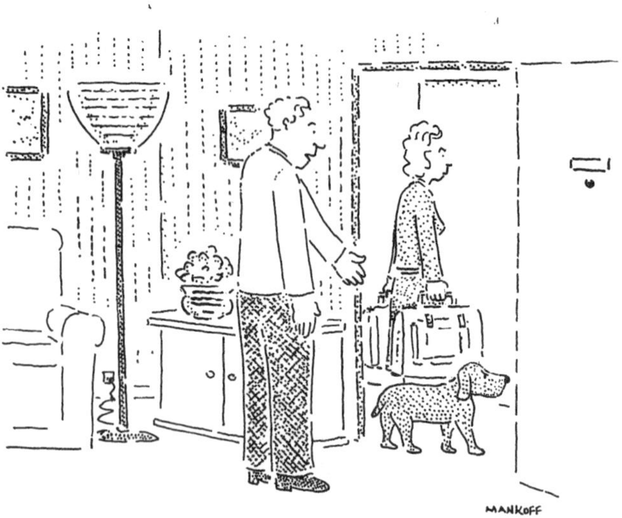
MANKOFF

"Et tu, Baxter?"

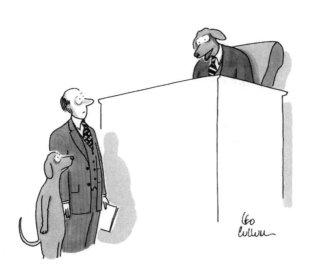

"I'm going to disqualify myself."

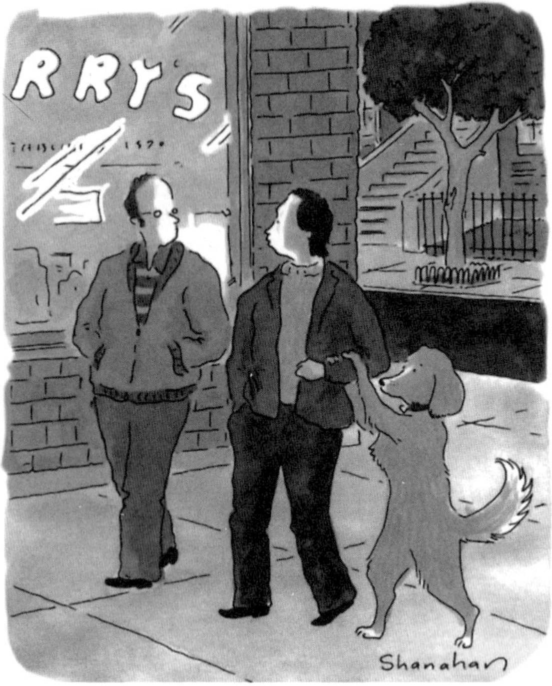
RRY'S
Shanahan

"She never took to the leash."

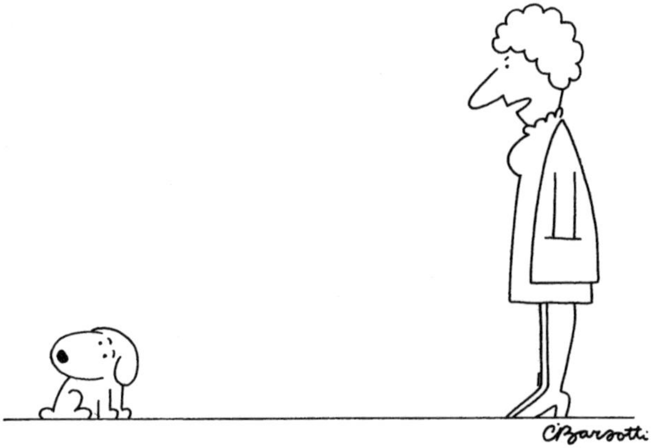
CBarsotti

"Yes, I'm talking to you. I believe you're the only Sparky in the house."

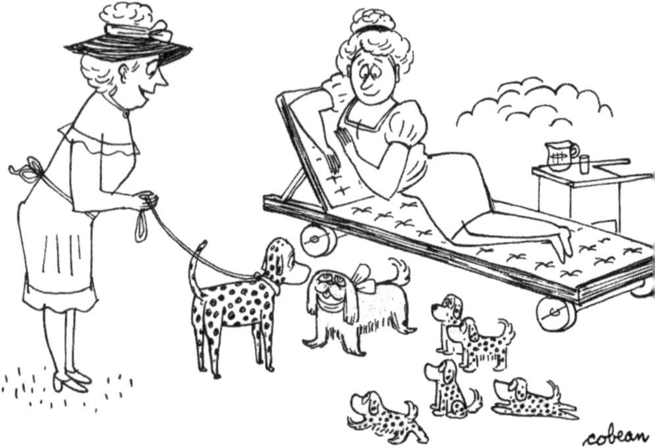
cobean

"You remember Trixie, don't you, Freddie?"

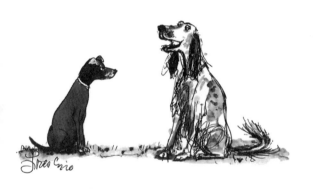

"They never pushed me. If I wanted to retrieve, shake hands, or
roll over, it was entirely up to me."

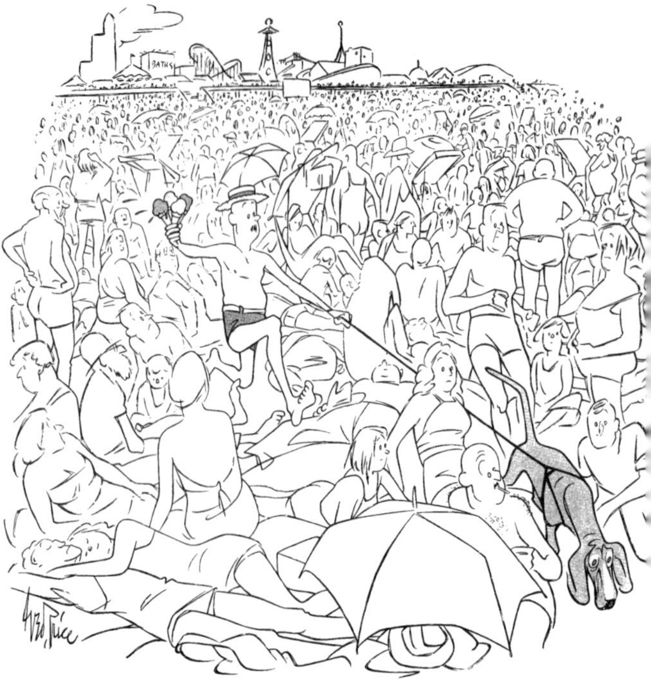
BATHS

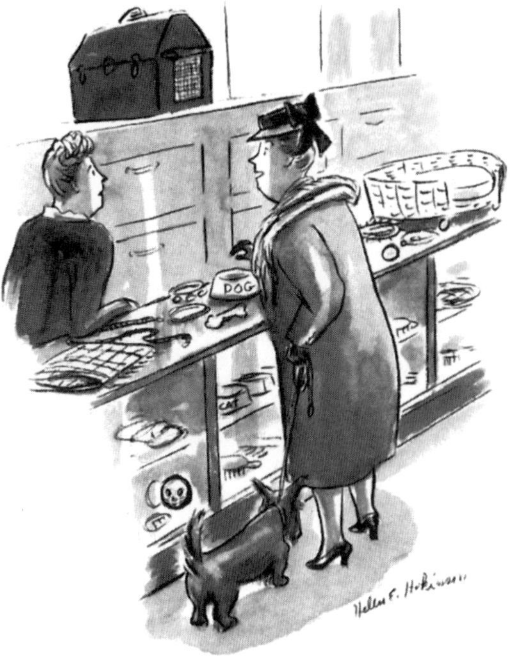
DOG
CAT

"We want to send a hostess present to a dachshund."

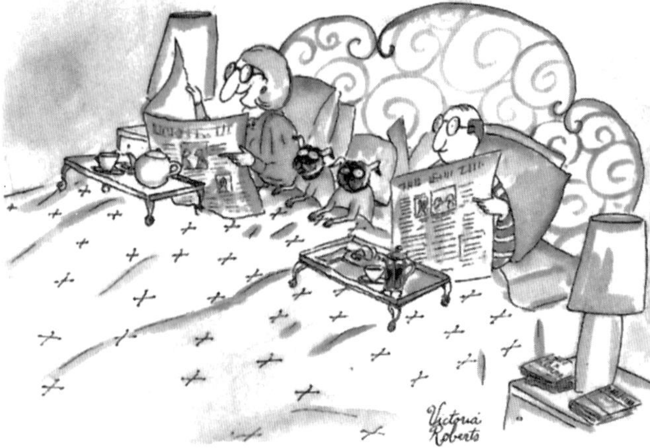
Victoria Roberts

"If you lie down with pugs, you wake up with pugs."

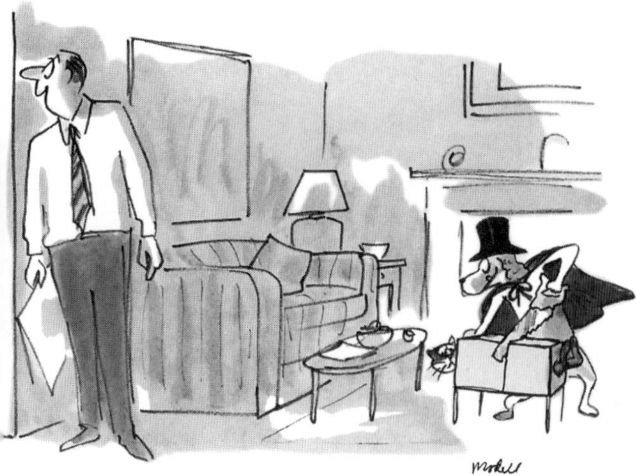

"Come here a minute, dear. Skeeter's learned a new trick."

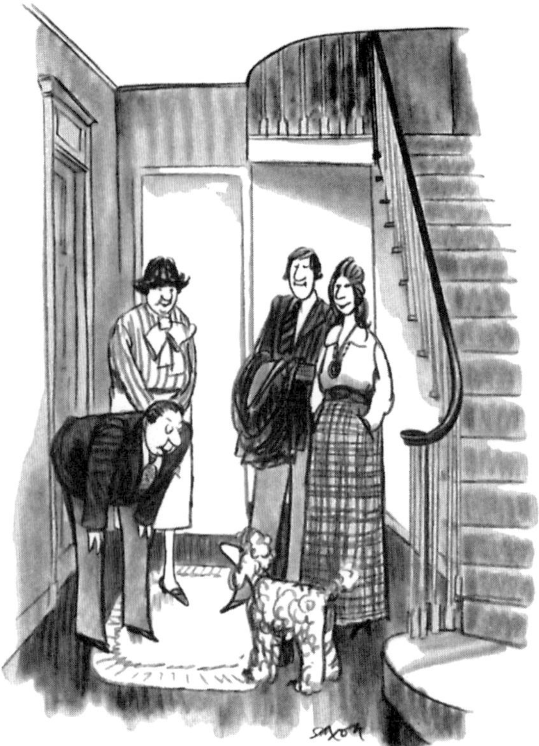

"And <u>this</u>, I presume, is Fluffy?"

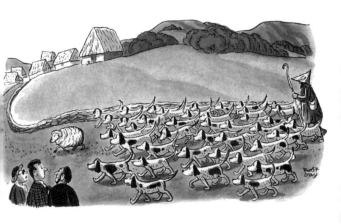

"*I understand that in your country this thing is done
quite differently.*"

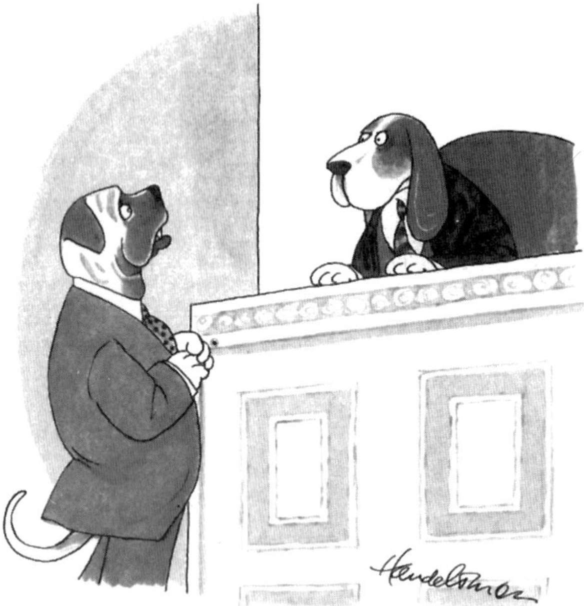

"I didn't realize, Your Honor. I assumed the law here was the same as in New Jersey. As you may know, dog eat dog is permissible there."

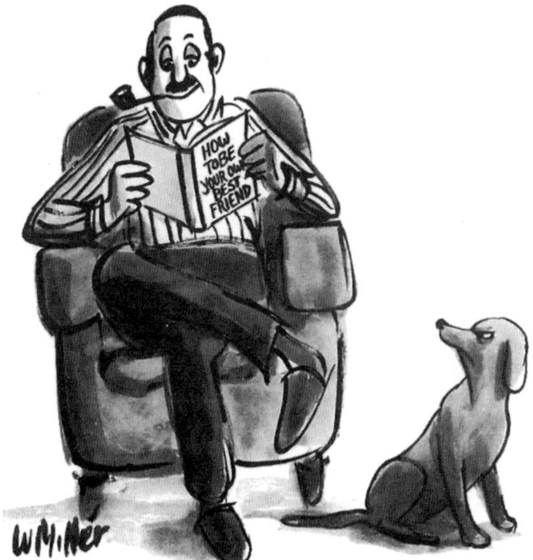
HOW
TO BE
YOUR OWN
BEST
FRIEND
W.Miller

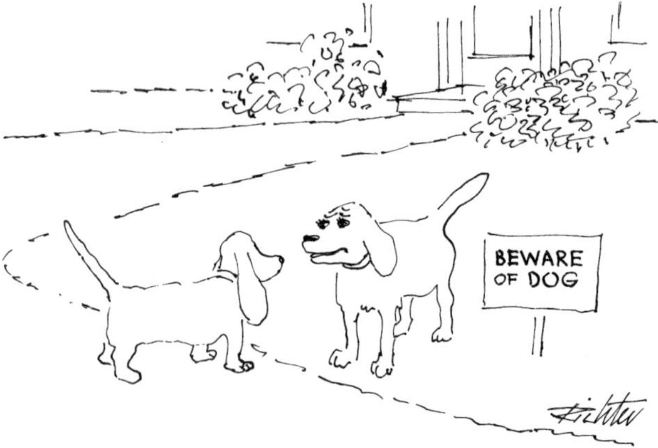
BEWARE
OF DOG
Richter

"It's very gratifying, but there's a lot of responsibility that goes along with it."

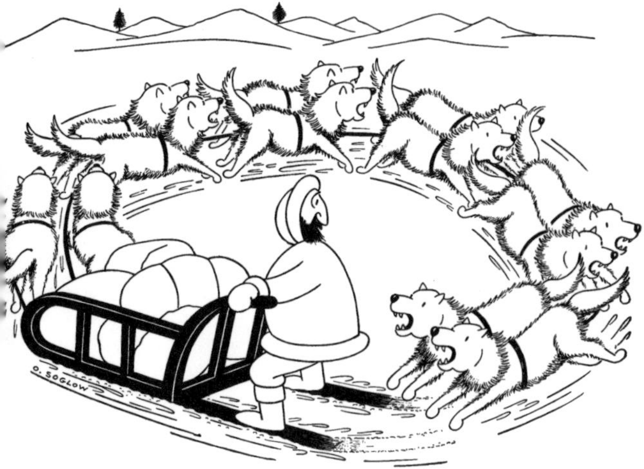
O. SOGLOW

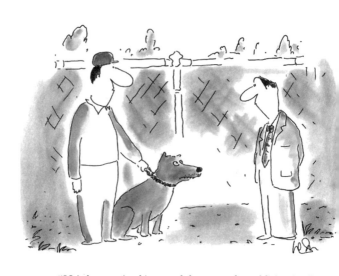

"He's been trained in guard duty, attack, and litigation."

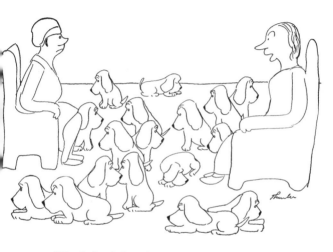

"The father belonged to some people who were driving through in a Packard."

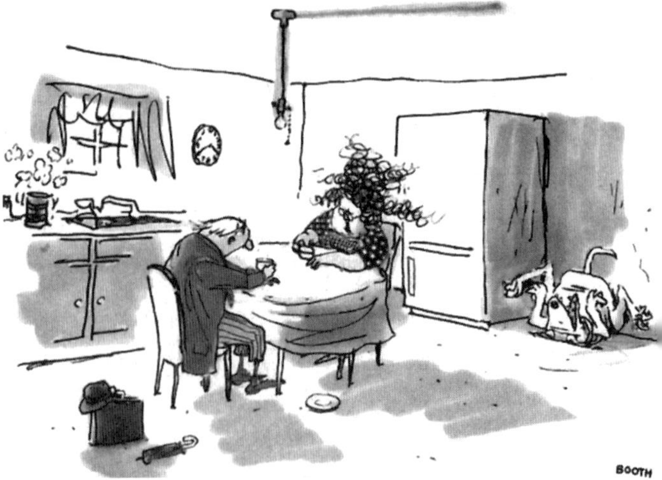
BOOTH

"Don't give the dog any more coffee."

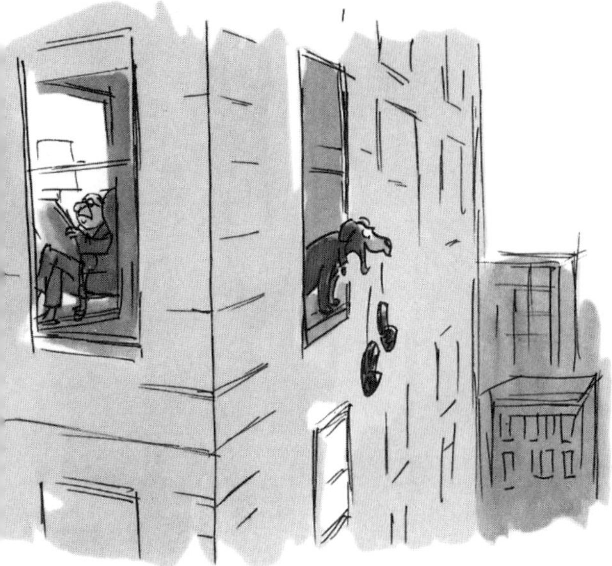

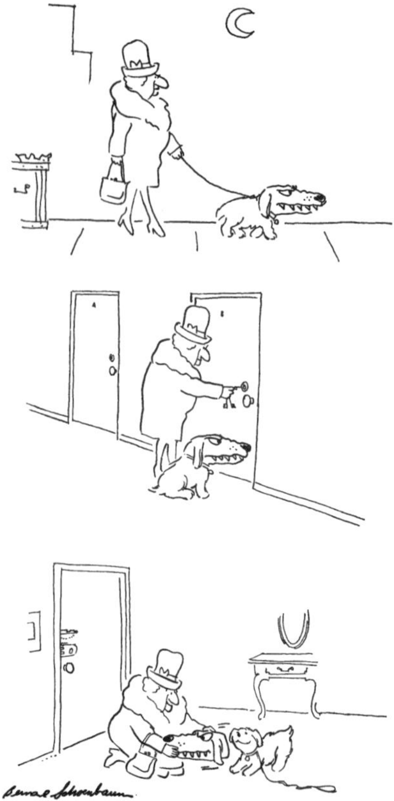

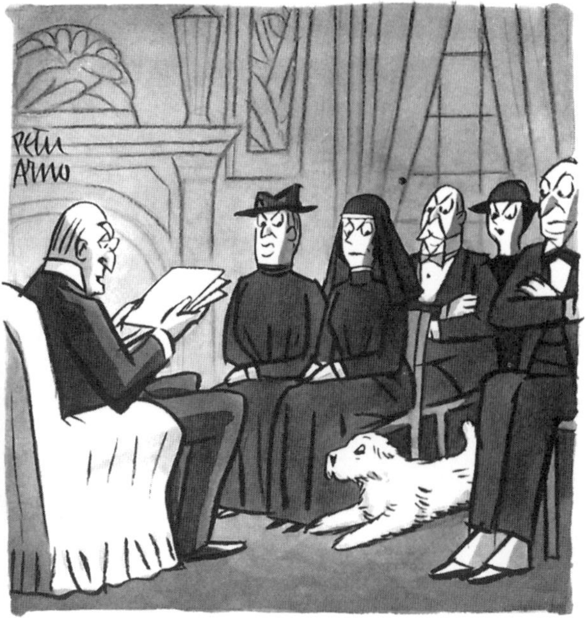
Peter Arno

"First then: the bulk of my estate, excepting certain specific bequests as hereinafter noted, I leave to my true friend and companion, one of God's noblest creatures . . ."

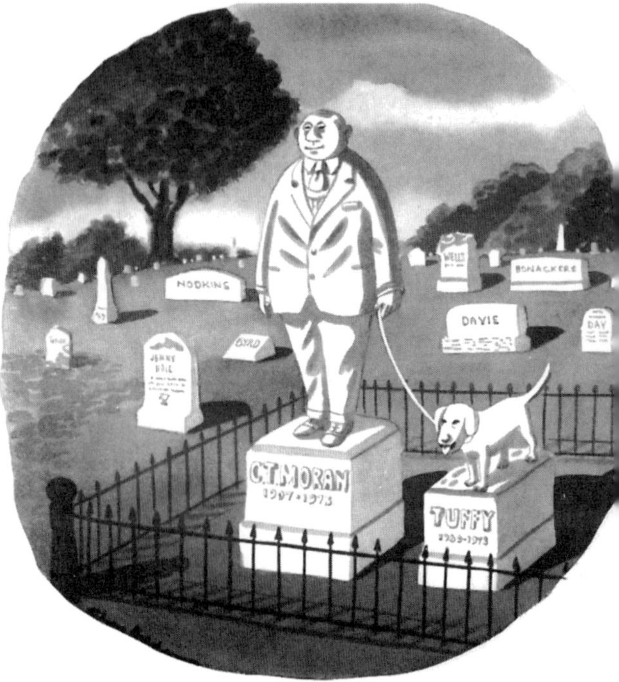
NODKINS
WELLS
BONACKERS
DAVIE
DAY
BYRD
C.T. MORAN
TUFFY

STEINBERG

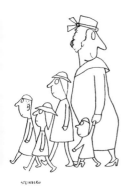

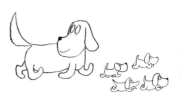

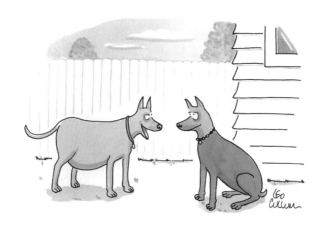

If it's girls, Kimberly, Kaitlin, Lauren, Cindy, and Tracy.
If it's boys, Cameron, Christopher, Adam, Jeffrey, and Gregory."

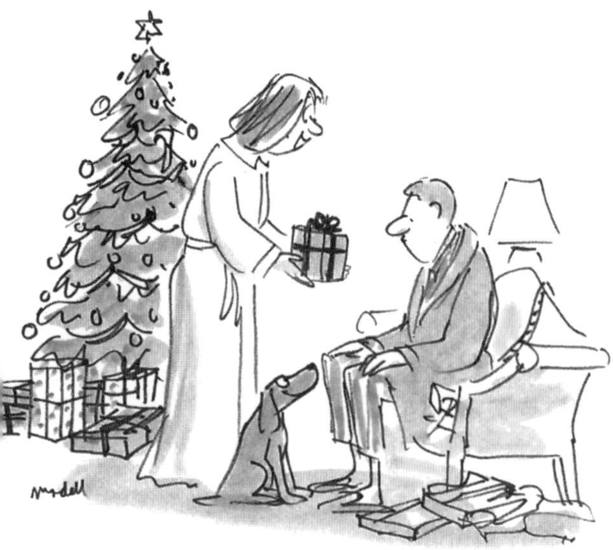

"This one's from you know who, so make a fuss and thank him."

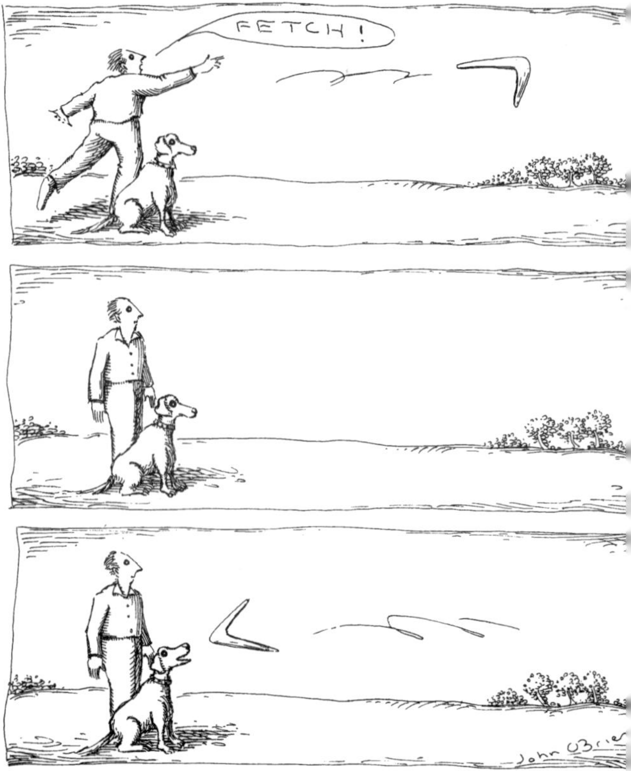
FETCH!
John O'Brien

CHILDREN OF CELEBRITY CANINES

BRITTANY:
Daughter of Lassie. Hopes to become an actress/model. Not completely without talent, but close.
LANCE:
Benji's offspring. At the moment, wants to be a rock-and-roll drummer. A borderline sociopathic ne'er-do-well.
SO WHATCHA LOOKIN' AT, HUH?
ROVER:
Son of Andalusian Dog. Happy and well adjusted. Nothing at all like his dad.

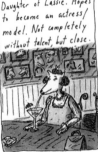

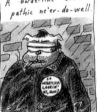

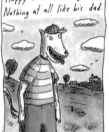

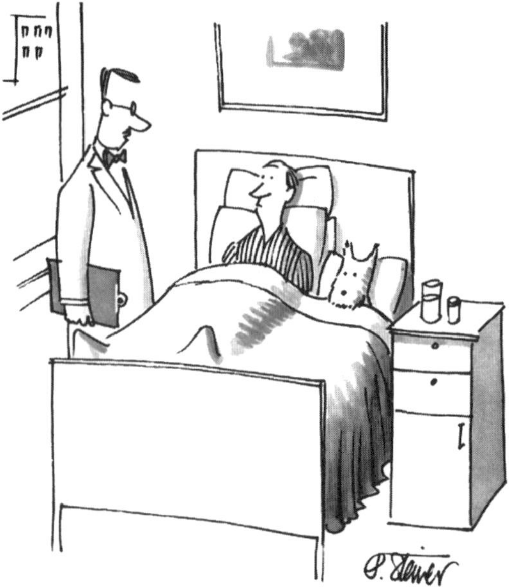

"Under our holistic approach, Mr. Wyndot, we not only treat your symptoms, we also treat your dog."

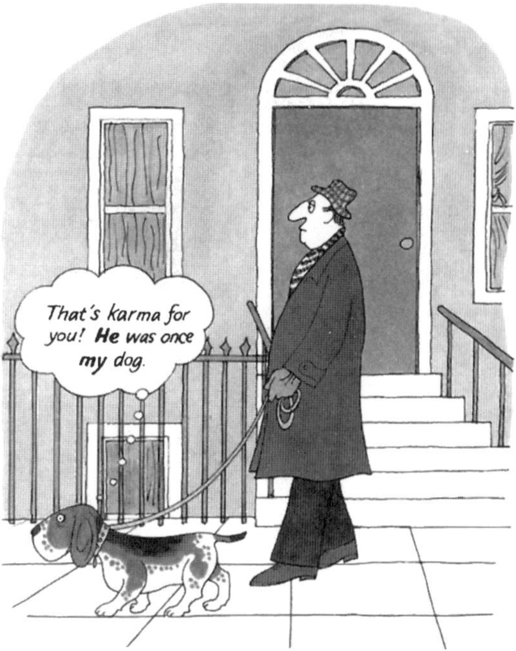
That's karma for you! He was once my dog.

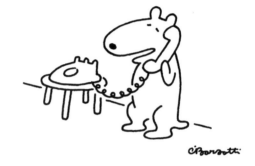

"Well, please look again, Operator. It's Fluffy—
F-L-U-F-F-Y—and she lives in Larchmont."

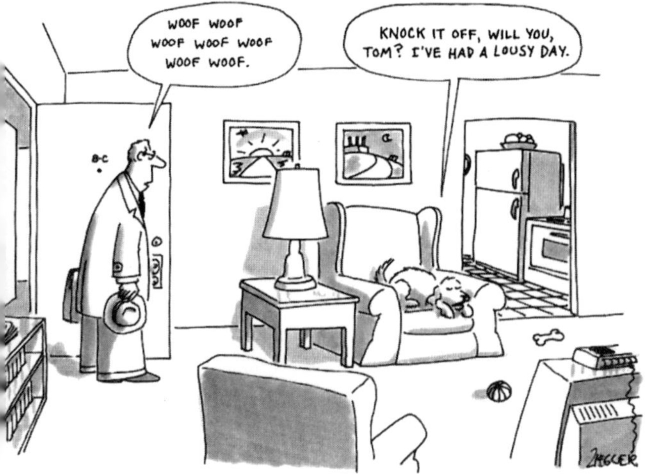
WOOF WOOF
WOOF WOOF WOOF
WOOF WOOF.
KNOCK IT OFF, WILL YOU,
TOM? I'VE HAD A LOUSY DAY.

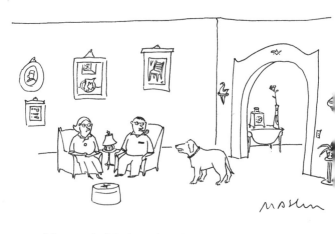

"Once again I find myself in the rather awkward position of
having to ask one of you for a biscuit."

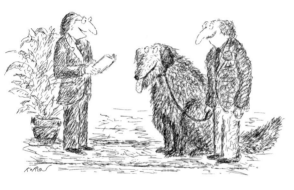

"Do you, Daisy, promise to love, honor, and, in particular, obey Mr. Singer? To beg, sit, stay, heel, and roll over until death do you part?"

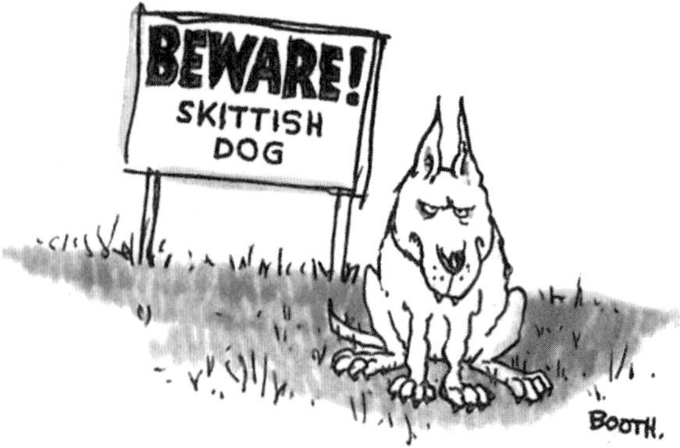
BEWARE!
SKITTISH
DOG
BOOTH.

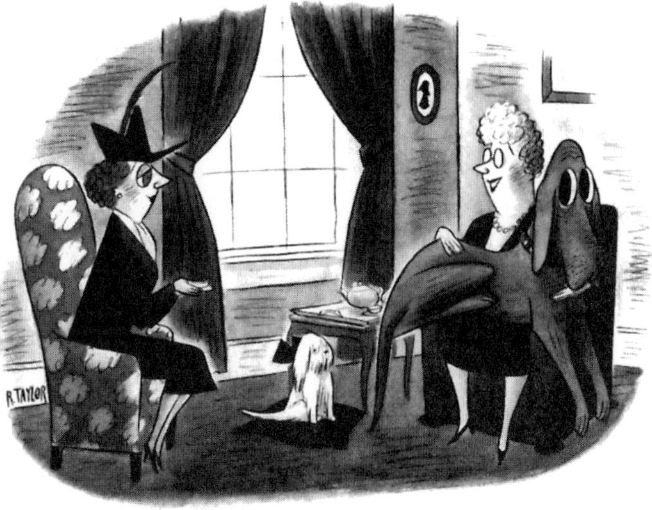
R. TAYLOR

"He's terribly jealous of Fifi."

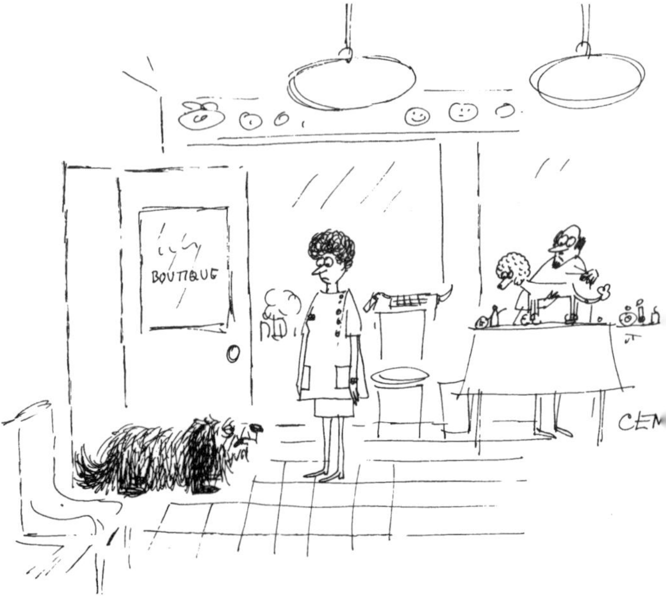
BOUTIQUE

"The works."

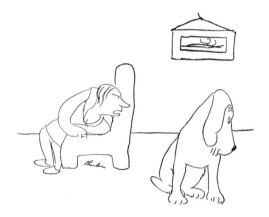

"You ought to spend more time with your own species."

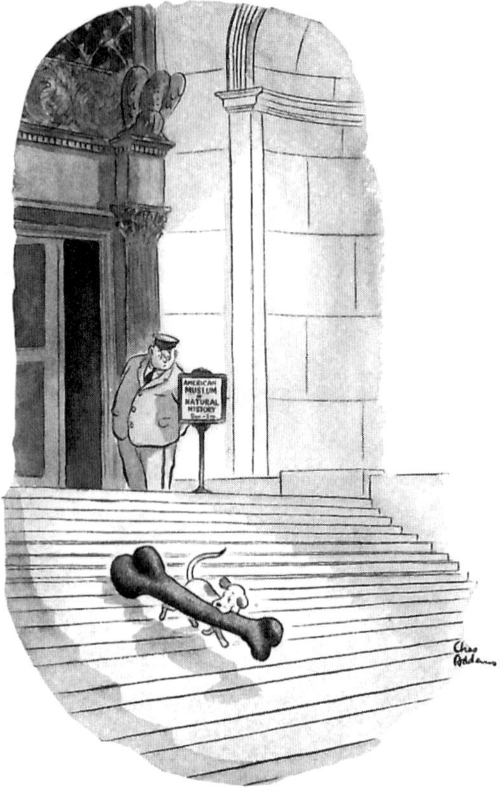
AMERICAN
MUSEUM
NATURAL
HISTORY
Chas Addams

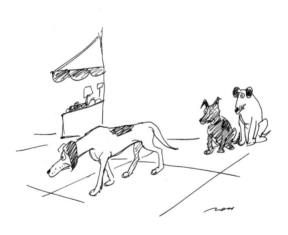

"It's a shame. He's lost the will to fetch."

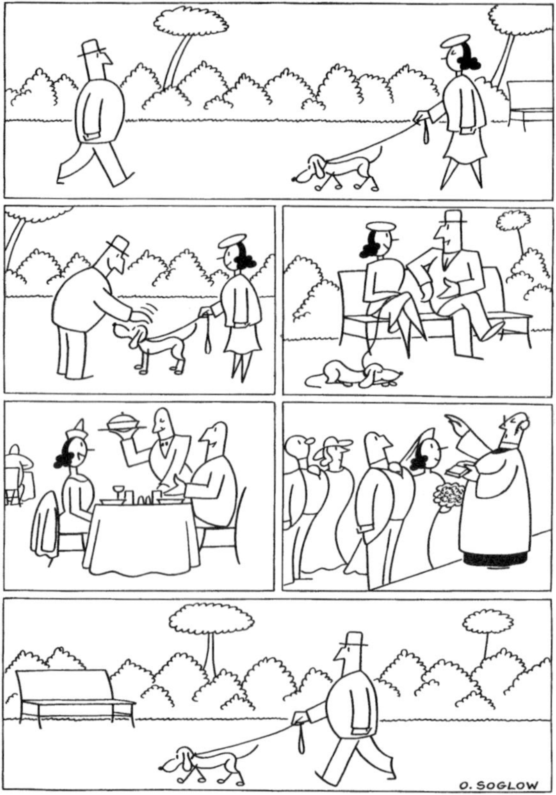
O. SOGLOW

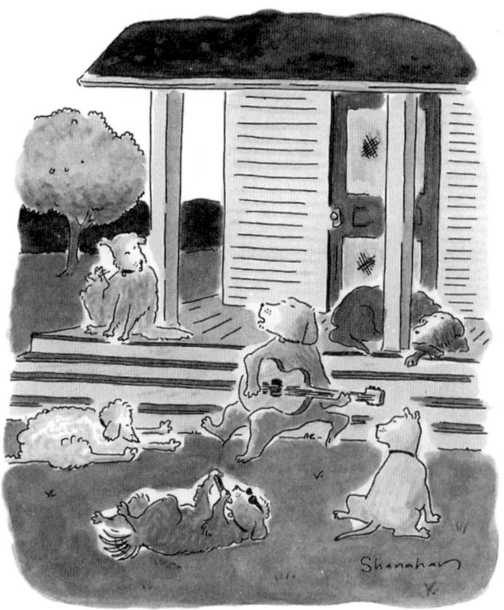
Shanahan

"'I'm a good dog, Mama, I'll bring you your daily news.
I'm a good dog, Mama, I don't chew my master's shoes.
But there's one thing life has learnt me—even good dogs get the blues.'
Blow some sweet harp for me, Lucky."

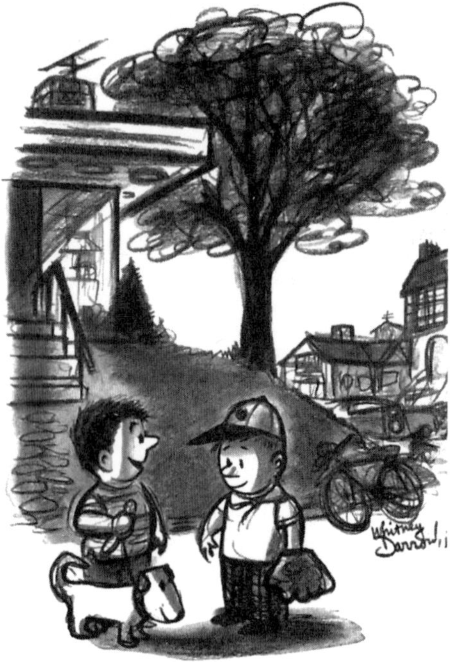
Whitney Darrow, Jr.

"He's only four weeks old, and he can already say 'arf.'"

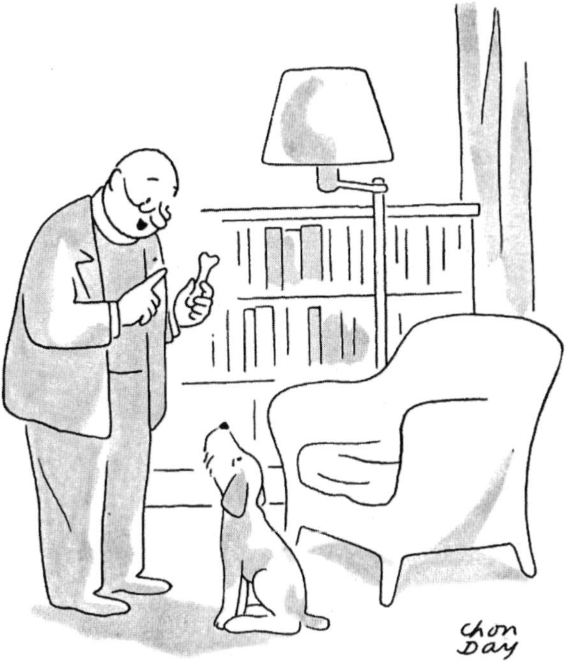
Chon Day

"Pray for it."

THE BLOODHOUND AND THE BUG

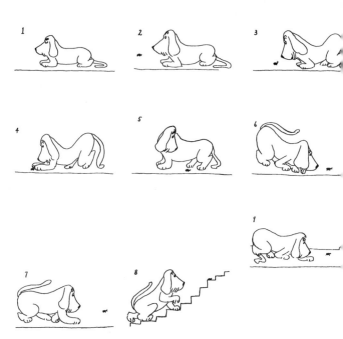

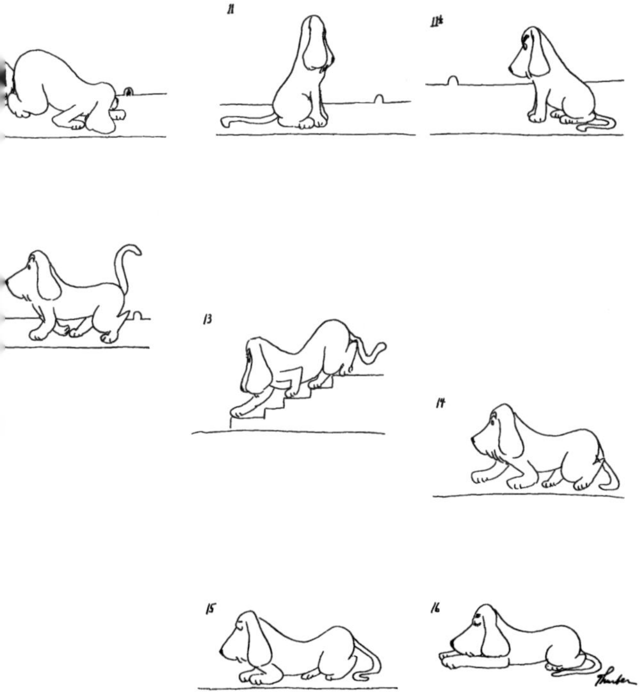
11
11½
13
14
15
16
Thurber

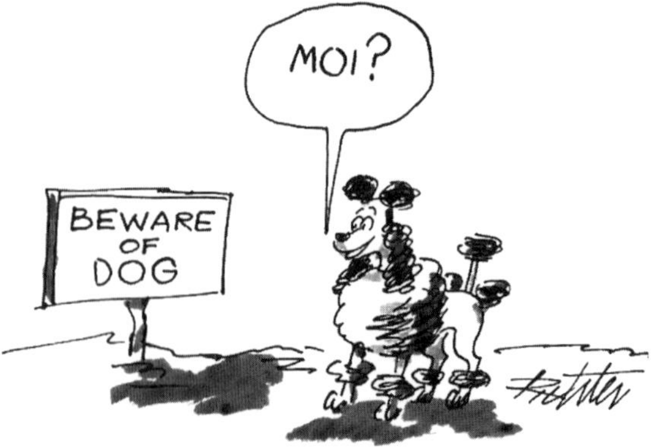
MOI?
BEWARE OF DOG

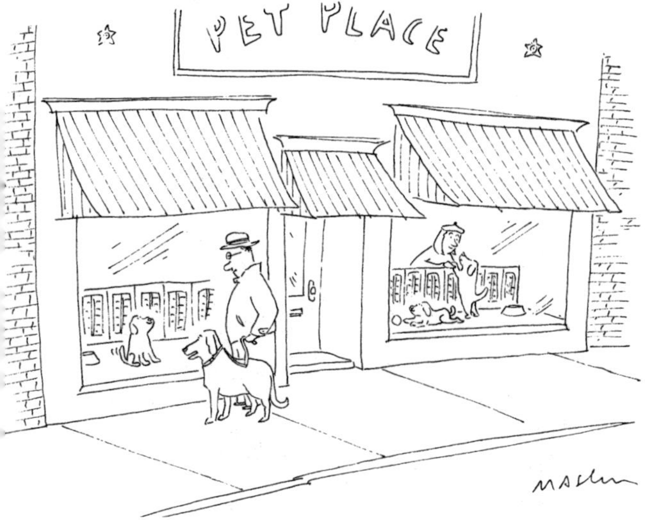
PET PLACE

"He is cute, but you already have a dog."

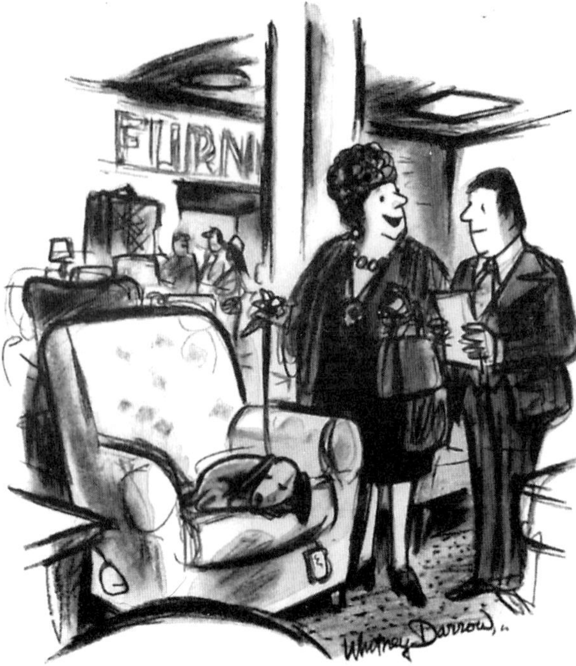
FURN
Whitney Darrow, Jr.

"Sold!"

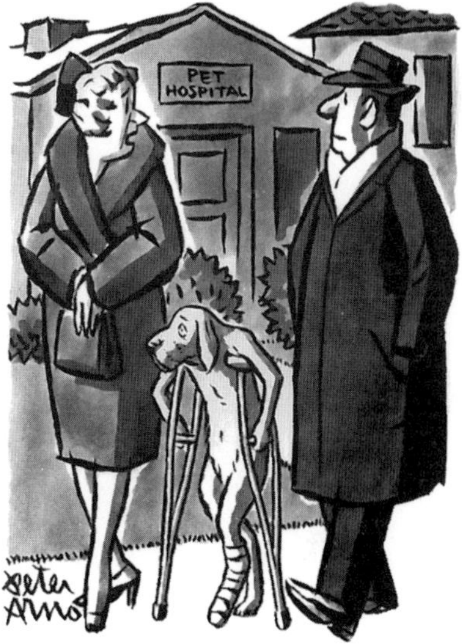
PET
HOSPITAL
Peter
Arno

"He may be a fine veterinarian, but we're going to get some funny looks."

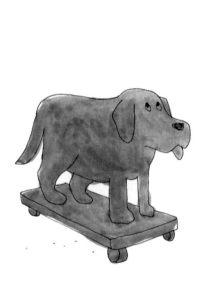
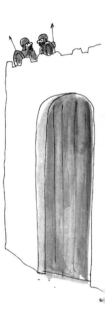

"I think the Greeks are running out of ideas."

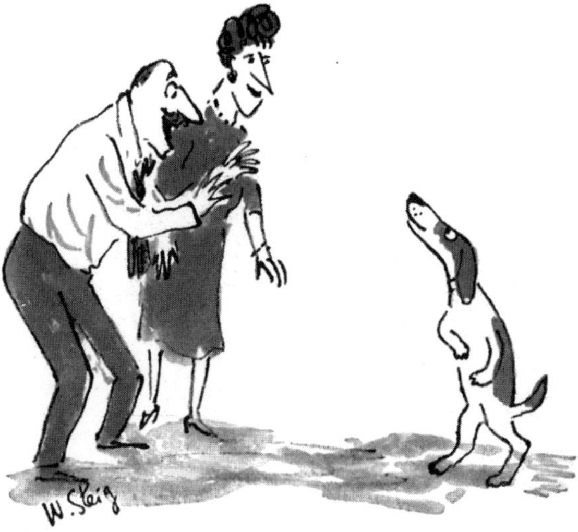
W. Steig

"He's got it! The Frug!"

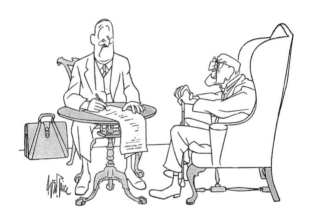

"...and the balance of my estate I want to put into a trust for the
care and maintenance of my most loyal friend and faithful
companion, my dog Spot. Now go out and get me a dog with spots."

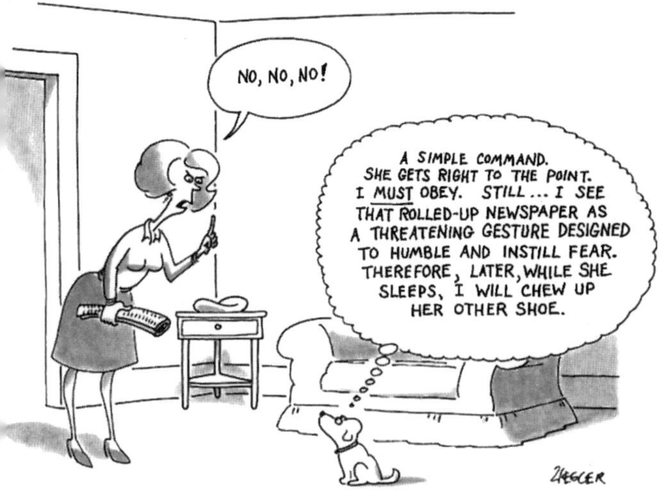
NO, NO, NO!
A SIMPLE COMMAND. SHE GETS RIGHT TO THE POINT. I MUST OBEY. STILL... I SEE THAT ROLLED-UP NEWSPAPER AS A THREATENING GESTURE DESIGNED TO HUMBLE AND INSTILL FEAR. THEREFORE, LATER, WHILE SHE SLEEPS, I WILL CHEW UP HER OTHER SHOE.
ZIEGLER

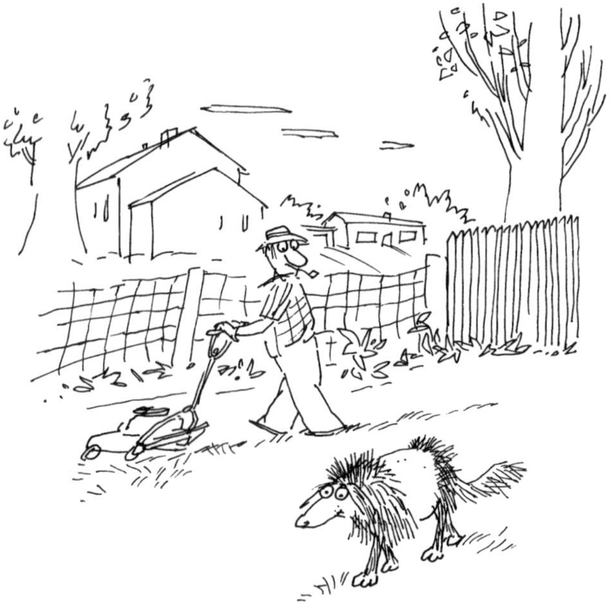

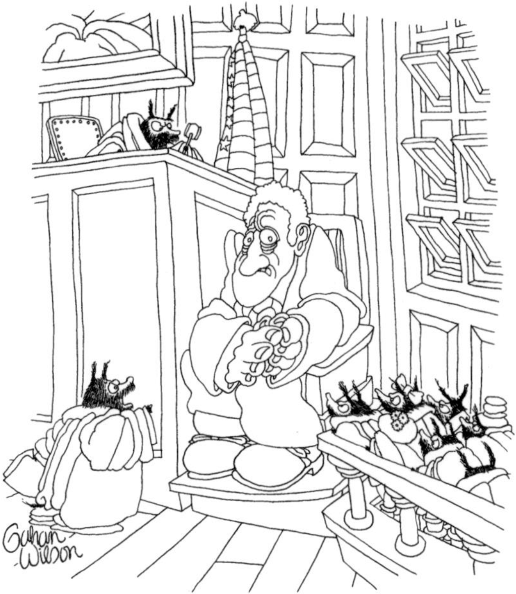
Gahan Wilson

"Did you or did you not employ a leash to drag your cairn terrier, Jack, away from the corner of Park Avenue and Sixty-fifth Street in spite of his making every effort to clearly indicate to you that he wished to stay where he was?"

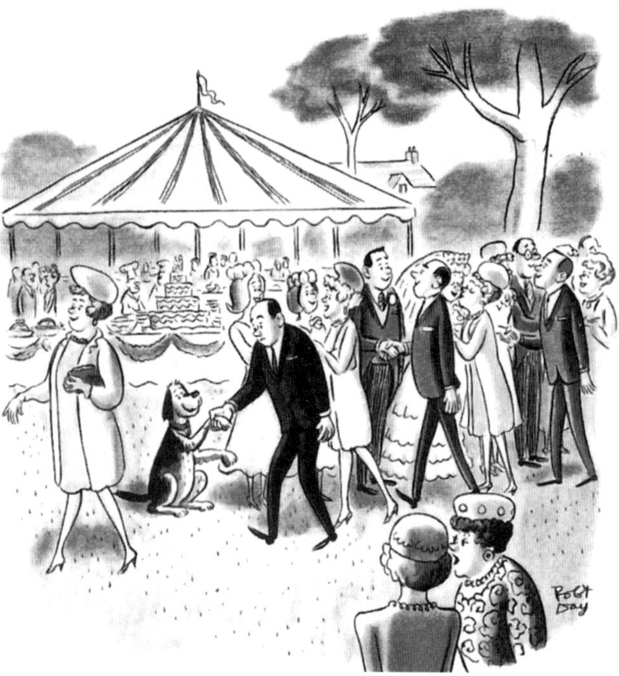
Robt Day

"Well, they consider him a member of the family."

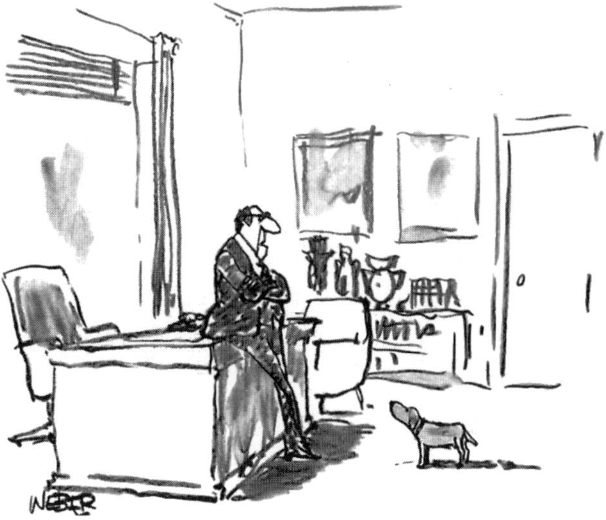
WEBER

"I'll lay it out for you. We're cutting back, and we no longer need a dog."

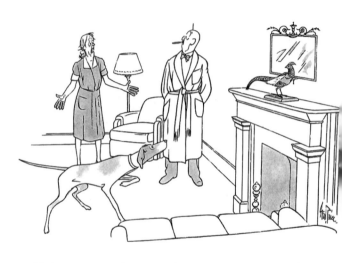

"You've got to get rid of one or the other. It's getting on my nerves."

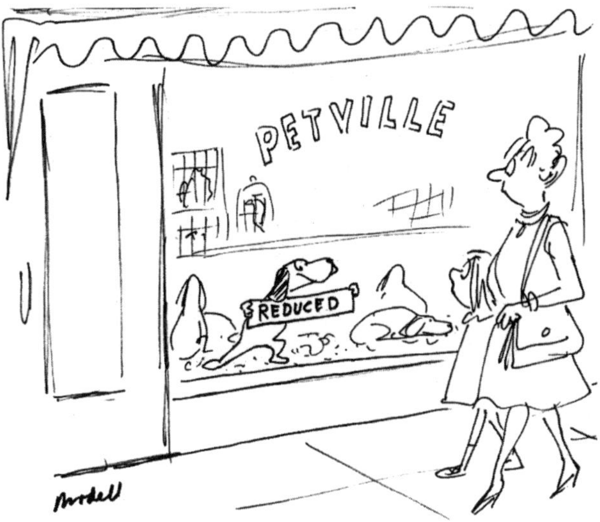
PETVILLE
REDUCED
Modell

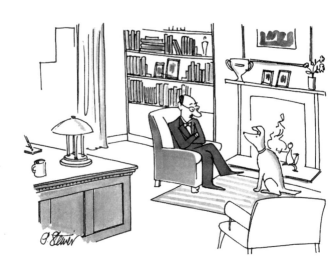

"I've told you why I need a dog. Now suppose you tell me what makes you think you might be that dog."

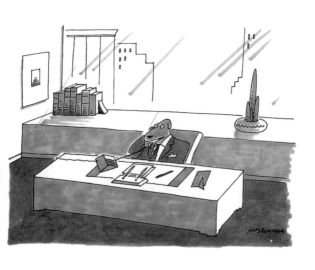

"Woof woof woof woof!... I mean, get me the Techcorp file, Thompson."

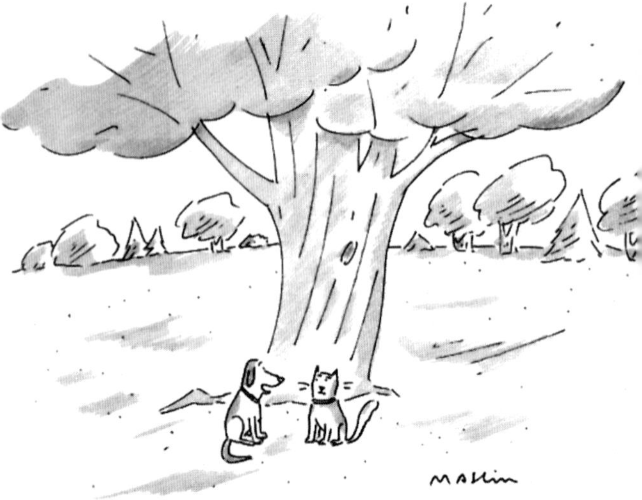
MAslin

"You realize I'm taking an enormous personal as well as professional risk just being seen with you."

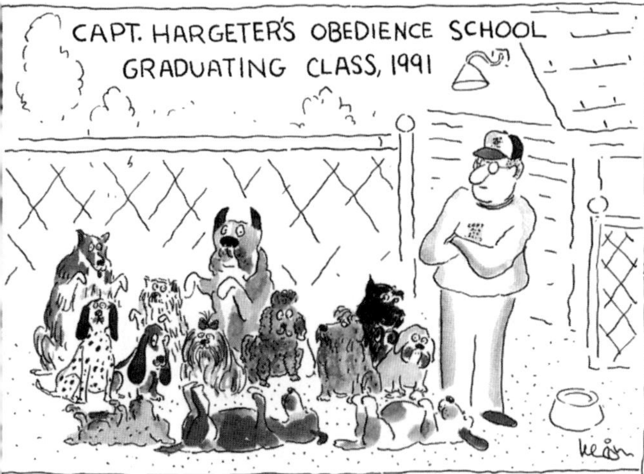
CAPT. HARGETER'S OBEDIENCE SCHOOL
GRADUATING CLASS, 1991

PLAYING DEAD: MUFFY, PRINCE, BOBO. STANDING: CAPT. HARGETER. SITTING: SPOT, GORBY, TOFU, FLUFFY, TERRY, BUSTER. BEGGING: OREO, TOTO, RAMBO, SCOTTIE. NOT SHOWN (FETCHING): TOBY, TUTU, ROXIE.

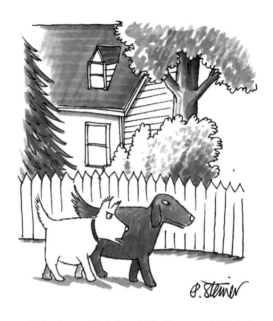

"It's always 'Sit,' 'Stay,' 'Heel'—never 'Think,'
'Innovate,' 'Be yourself.'"

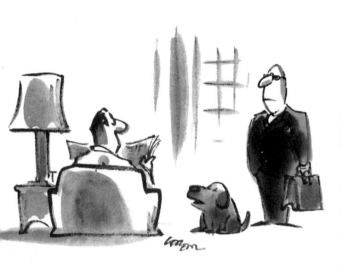

*"From now on, Ted, I will speak only when
adequately represented by counsel."*

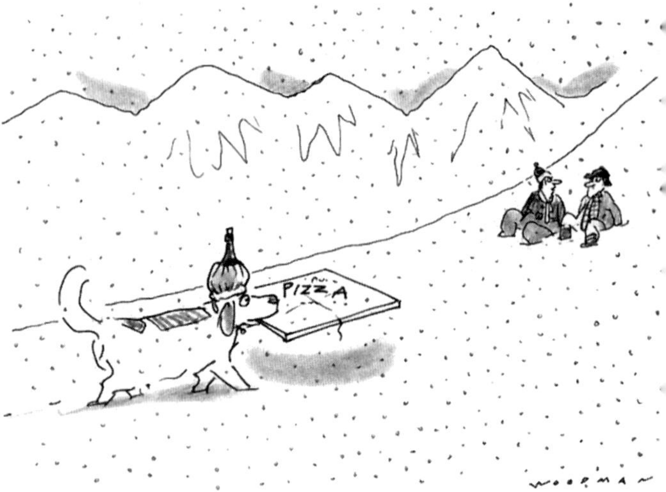
PIZZA
WOODMAN

"We must be in the Italian Alps."

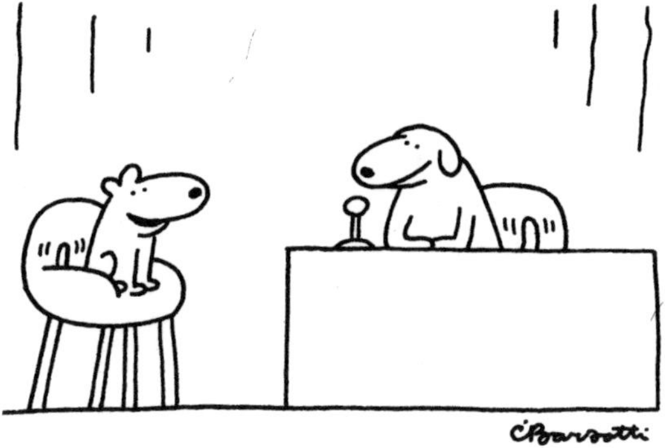
C Barsotti

"And I'm happy to be here, Johnny."

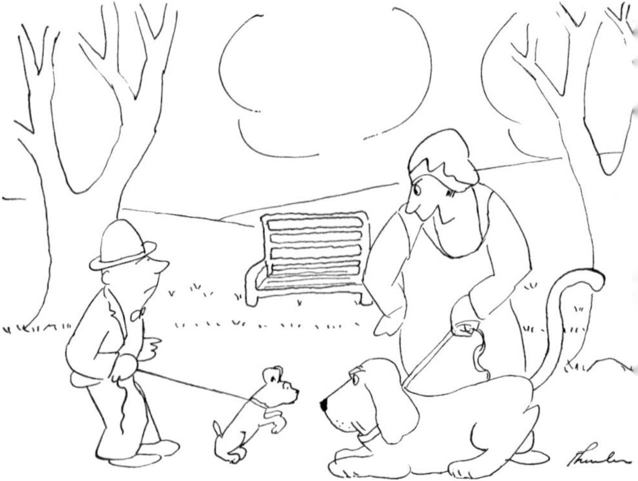

"Are you two looking for trouble, Mister?"

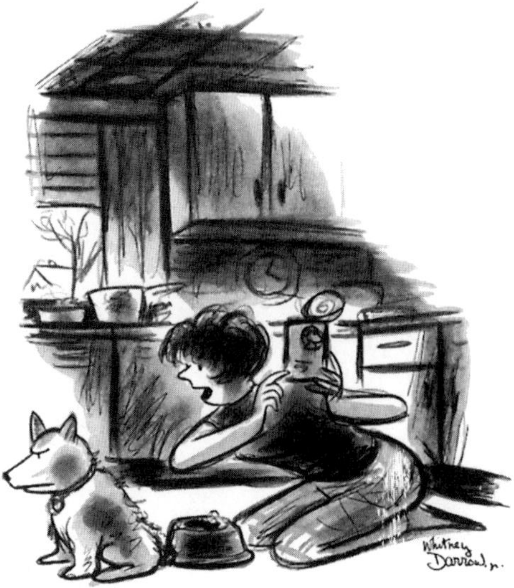
Whitney Darrow, Jr.

"Now, look! It says right here on the can how good this is for you: commended by veterinarians everywhere. Beef livers appetizingly ooked in their own juices. Vitamin C added. Contains minimum daily requirement of riboflavin . . .' "

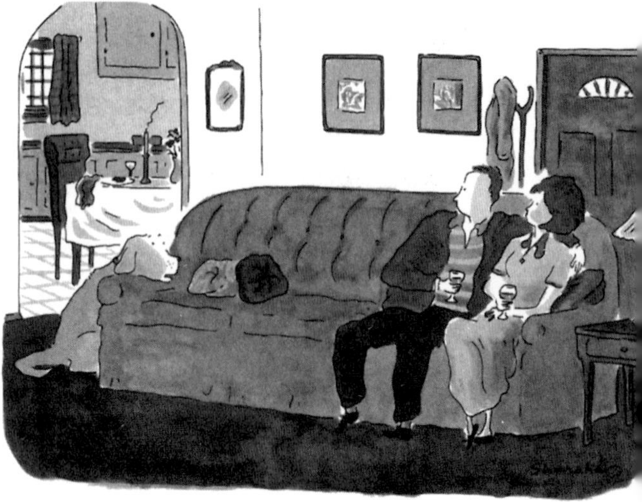

"If you two are through with your braised sirloin tips, I'll just go ahead and clear the table."

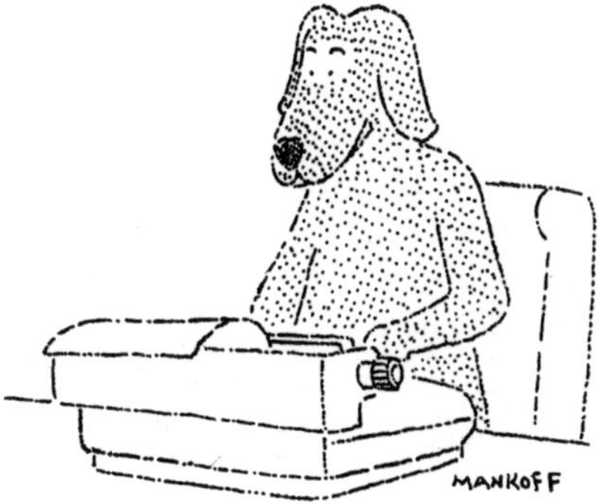
MANKOFF

"The quick brown dog jumps over the lazy fox."

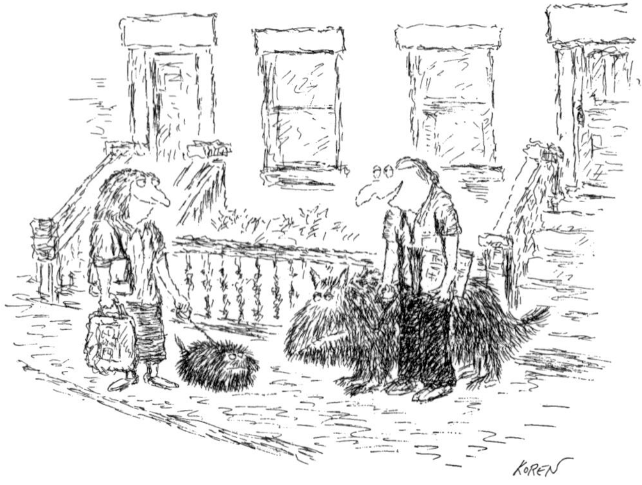
KOREN

"How long have you and Charlie been together?"

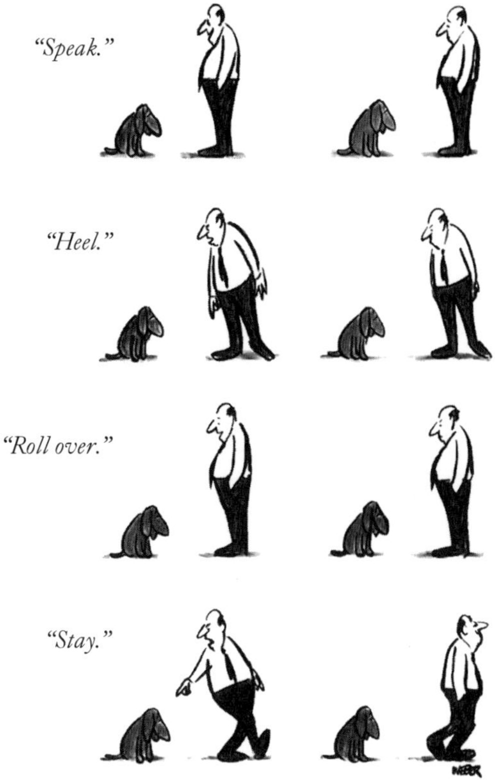
"Speak."
"Heel."
"Roll over."
"Stay."
WEBER

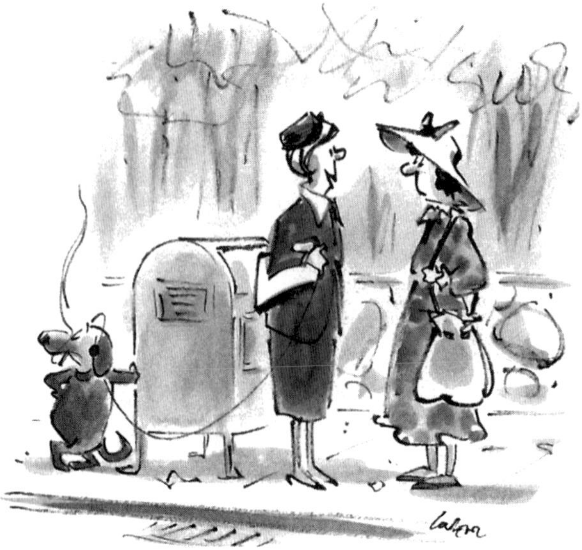

"I used to think it was cruel to keep a dog in the city, but Homer's made a remarkable adjustment."

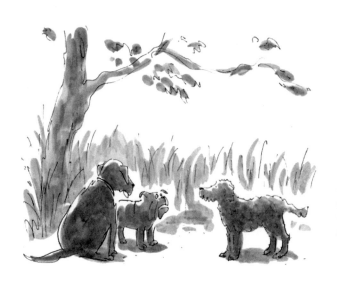

"Speaking personally, I haven't had my day, and I've never met any dog who has."

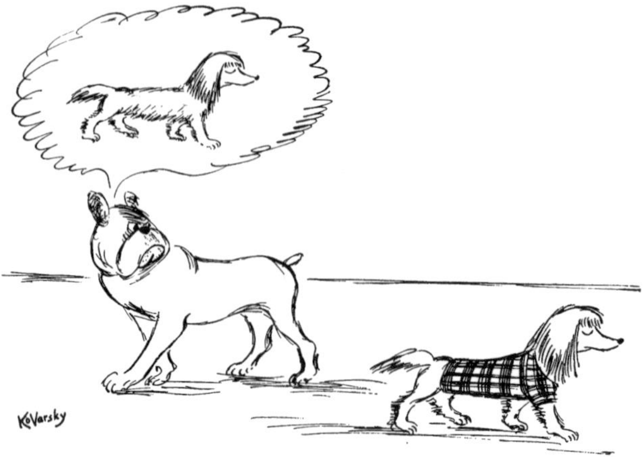
KoVarsky

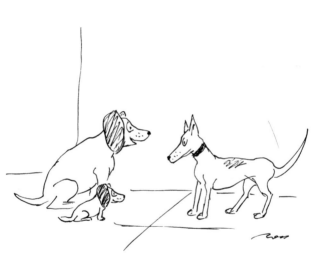

"He has my bite and his father's bark."

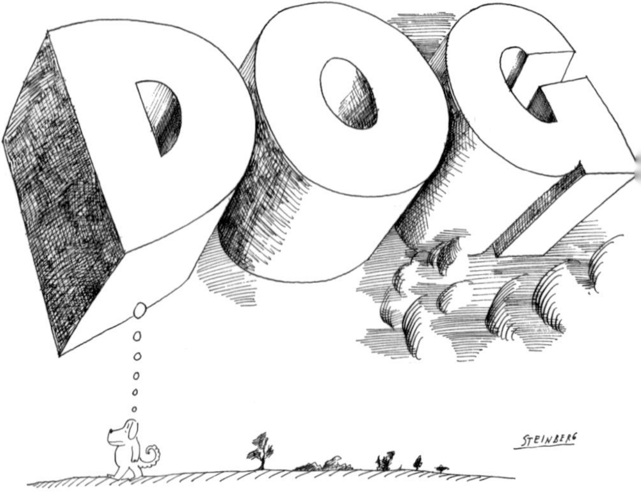
DOG
STEINBERG

Index of Artists

Charles Addams 9, 46, 62

Peter Arno 18, 45, 73

Charles Barsotti 5, 27, 54, 91

George Booth 6, 42, 58

Roz Chast 15, 51

Sam Cobean 28

Michael Crawford 8

Leo Cullum 10, 25, 48

Whitney Darrow, Jr. 66, 72, 93

Chon Day 67

Robert Day 35, 80

Eldon Dedini 23

Edward Frascino 29

Mort Gerberg 16

J. B. Handelsman 36, 53

Helen Hokinson 19, 31

Edward Koren 57, 96

Antole Kovarsky 100

Arnie Levin 12, 40, 87

Lee Lorenz 89, 98

Robert Mankoff 24, 95

Charles E. Martin 60

Michael Maslin 20, 56, 71, 86

Warren Miller 37

Frank Modell 33, 49, 83

John O'Brien 14, 50

George Price 14, 30, 76, 82

Mischa Richter 38, 70

Victoria Roberts 32

Al Ross 1, 22, 63, 101

Charles Saxon 34

Bernard Schoenbaum 11, 44

Danny Shanahan 4, 26, 65, 94

Otto Soglow 39, 64

Edward Sorel 17

William Steig 2, 21, 75

Saul Steinberg 13, 47, 102

Peter Steiner 54, 84, 88

Mick Stevens 85

James Stevenson 43, 74, 99

Richard Taylor 59

James Thurber 3, 41, 61, 68—9, 92

Robert Weber 7, 81, 97

Gahan Wilson 79

Bill Woodman 78, 90

Jack Ziegler 55, 77

The text of this book was set in a postscript version of Caslon Old Face No. 2. Designed by Virginia Tan